This book is to
the las.

D1549182

For Julia – SG
To Steven, Jane, Drew, Josie and Isabelle with love – SA

First published in Great Britain in 1999 by Macdonald Young Books

Reprinted in 2000 by Hodder Wayland,
an imprint of Hodder Children's Books

Hodder Children's Books
A division of Hodder Headline
338 Euston Road
London NW1 3BH
Concept and design by Liz Black
Commissioning Editor Dereen Taylor
Editor Rosie Nixon
Language Consultant Betty Root
Science Consultant Dr Carol Ballard

Text © Sam Godwin
Illustrations © Simone Abel
Book © Hodder Wayland 1999
M.Y.Bees artwork © Clare Mackie

A CIP catalogue record for this book
is available from the British Library

ISBN   07500 2654 5

Printed and bound in Asa, Portugal

The case of the Missing Caterpillar

A first look at the life cycle of a butterfly

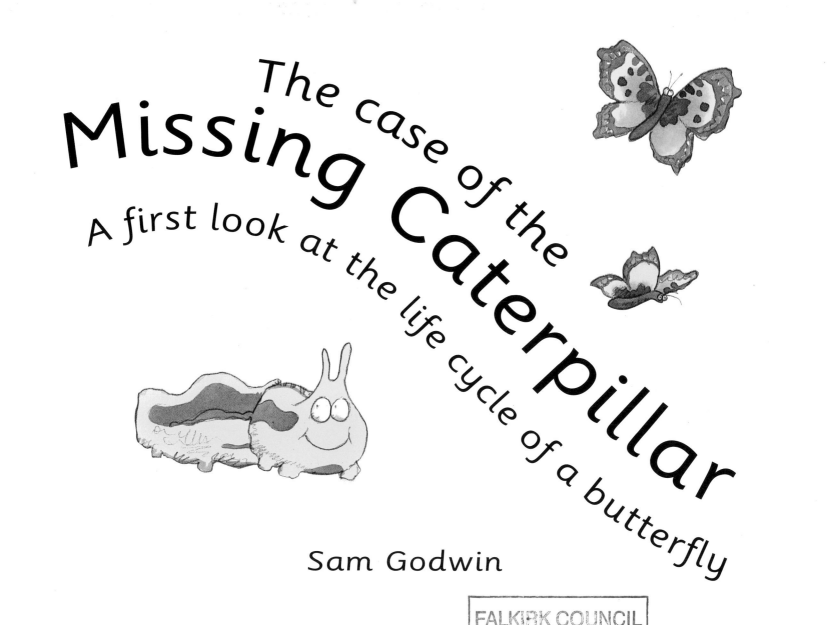

The case of the Missing Caterpillar

A first look at the life cycle of a butterfly

Sam Godwin

HODDER
Wayland

an imprint of Hodder Children's Books

It is springtime. There is a cluster of eggs

hidden under a leaf.

I don't know, but they've been there for about ten days.

Hey, look at that friendly caterpillar over there.

The eggs hatch and

8

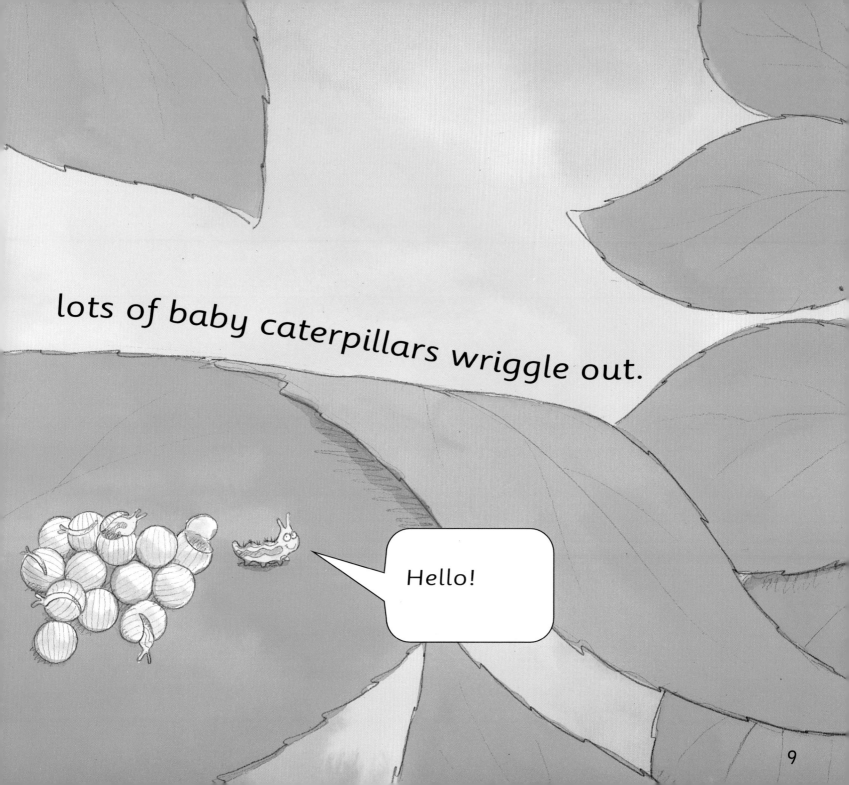

lots of baby caterpillars wriggle out.

Hello!

The caterpillars follow each other to the top of a plant.

The nest will protect the caterpillars from bad weather and hungry birds.

They all make a silk nest to hide in.

11

The caterpillar is very hungry. It munches nettles

If that caterpillar munches any more leaves it will pop!

12

and grows bigger and bigger...

13

That will keep on happening you know.

it grows too big for its skin!

15

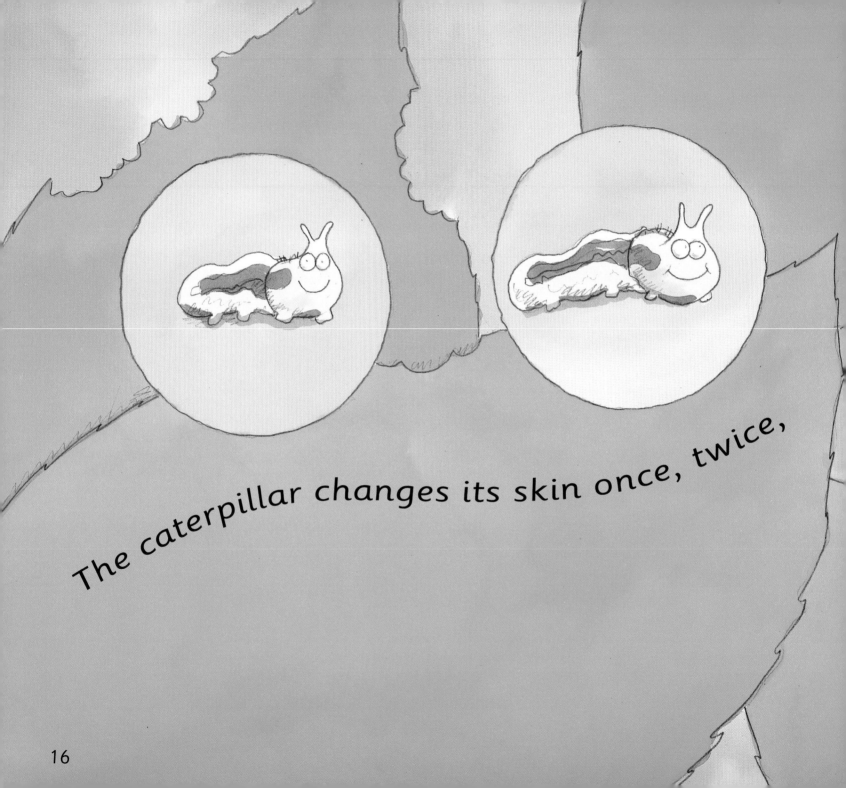

The caterpillar changes its skin once, twice,

three times.

I wish I could change my shell like that!

Hey, the caterpillar's disappeared! Where has it gone?

Now, all alone, the grown-up caterpillar

curls up in a leaf.

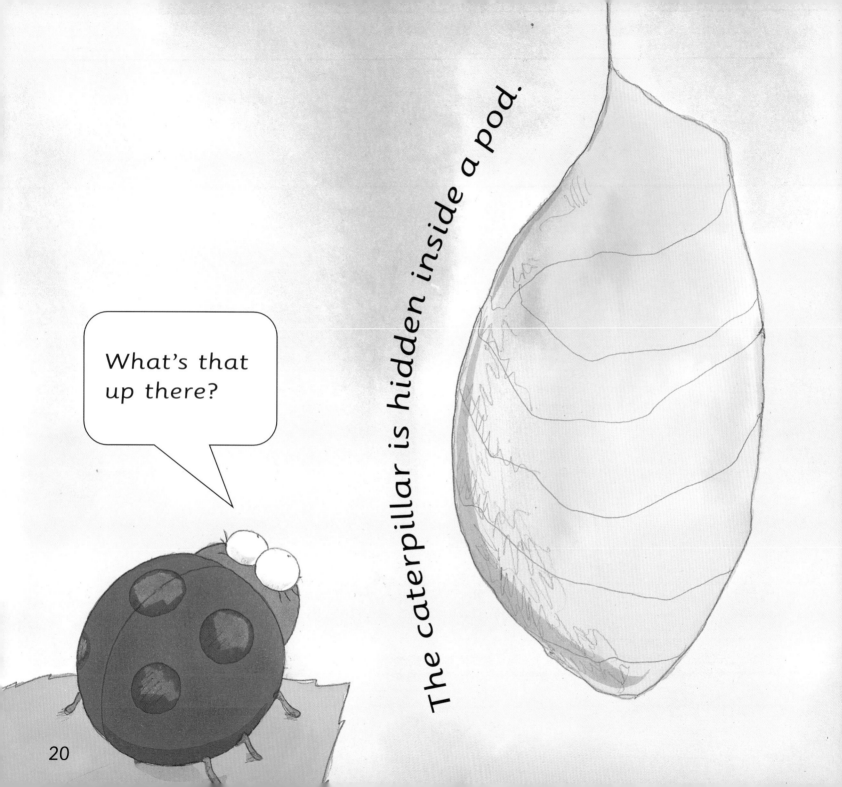

The caterpillar is hidden inside a pod.

20

For a while, all is quiet. Then, quite suddenly,

How long does it take for the chrysalis to open?

It depends on what kind of butterfly it is. Some open after only two weeks, some can stay closed for two years. This one's taken...

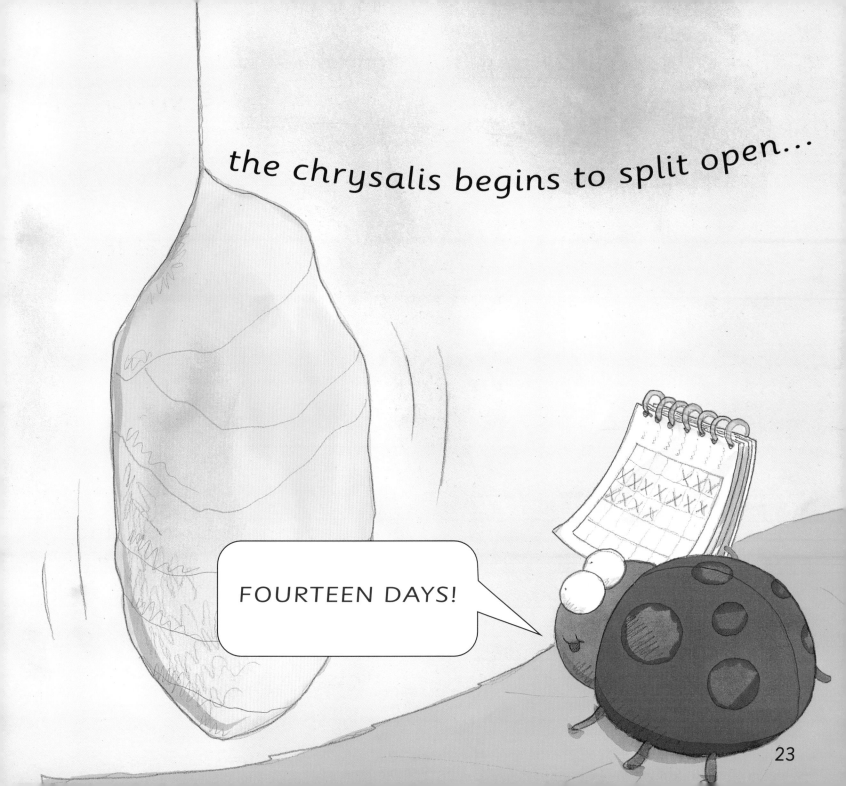

the chrysalis begins to split open...

FOURTEEN DAYS!

and a beautiful butterfly climbs out!

After a while, the butterfly stretches its wings

Wow! Look at its colourful wings.

26

and flies off into the sky.

It's so beautiful!

Four weeks later, the grown-up butterflies lay

I can't wait for these eggs to hatch.

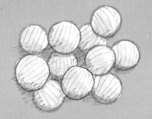

more eggs. The adventure begins all over again.

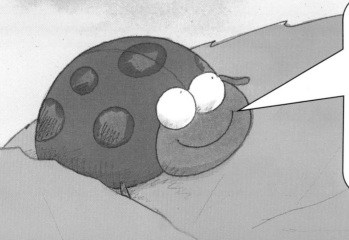

Yes, but this time we'll know where the missing caterpillar is!

Useful words

Hatch
To come out of an egg.

Nest
The home of insects, birds or animals. Some creatures are born in the nest.

Nettle
A big weed with prickly leaves.

Chrysalis
The pod or case inside which a caterpillar changes into a butterfly.

Pod
A kind of shell or case, like a chrysalis.

The Butterfly Life Cycle

(1) A grown-up butterfly lays some eggs under a leaf.

(7) The chrysalis splits open and a new butterfly comes out of it.

(2) The eggs hatch and little caterpillars wriggle out of them.

(6) The caterpillar turns into a chrysalis.

(5) The caterpillars all move out of the nest. From now on one caterpillar will live alone in a curled-up leaf.

(3) The caterpillars make a silk nest on top of a bush. They spend all their time nibbling on leaves.

(4) The caterpillars shed their skin.